A History of the

···

Family

❧

Compiled by

···

"To forget one's ancestors is to be a brook without a source, a tree without a root."

Chinese Proverb

Our Family History

Illustrated Edition

Tracing Your Family History

1. LIVING RELATIVES.

First-hand information is always the best. Your elderly relatives should be able to give you much information about their own families, their parents and grandparents, where they lived, what jobs they did and so on. Make a list of as many names as possible. They may have hoarded old documents, certificates and family photographs which will help you in your investigation.

2. OFFICIAL RECORDS

General Register Office: The General Register Office, located in St Catherine's House, Kingsway, London WC2B 6JP, holds records dating back to 1st July 1837 for England and Wales. There is no charge for searching the indexes.

You can request a copy of your own birth certificate, and from this you can work backwards, looking for both your parents' birth and marriage certificates, the marriage certificates of both sets of grandparents and so on. Once the entry has been found a full certificate can be supplied for a small fee.

Scottish Record Office: If you were born in Scotland you will need to consult the Scottish Record Office (PO Box 36, HM General Register House, Edinburgh EH1 3YY).

Local Parish Registers: For records of births, marriages and deaths before 1837 you will need to consult local parish registers which were first ordered to be kept in 1538. Not all parish registers have survived and many did not begin until the late 1600's. Most registers existing are in the hands of the clergy or locked for safe-keeping in the County or Diocesan Record Offices. Consulting these can be a lengthy process, especially in the larger cities, or if your family moved around the country a lot. However, there are some short-cuts. Phillimore and Co Ltd (Shopwyke Hall, Chichester, West Sussex PO20 6BQ) have published hundreds of parish registers thus minimizing the necessity for travelling all over the country. The Society of Genealogists (37 Harrington Gardens, London SW7 4JX) also holds many copies.

To trace your ancestors you will thus need to know which parish they were born in. You can search for this in the census returns.

3. CENSUS

A census has been taken every 10 years from 1801 and returns for 1841, 1851 and 1861 are housed in the Public Records Office (Land Registry Building, Portugal Street, London WC2A 1LR) and can be inspected by the general public. The census return gives information as to where each person was born, indicating which parish registers should be targeted for your searches.

4. OTHER DENOMINATIONS

Parish registers did not cover Dissentors, Foreigners and Jews. Sources for these groups can be found in the 12 volume National Index of Parish Registers published by Phillimore & Co. The Index includes records for the following groups: Nonconformists, Presbyterians, Independents, Baptists, Society of Friends, Moravians, Methodists, Foreign Churches, Roman Catholics and for Jewish Genealogy.

We wish you every success in your endeavour to trace your ancestors.

The Marriage

and

were joined together in marriage on

_at_

"An ideal wife is any woman who has an ideal husband."
Booth Tarkington

Our Genealogy

Husband's Full Name   ....

Birth Date   ....

Birth Place   ....

Father's Full Name   ....

Mother's Full Name   ....

Brothers & Sisters   ....

Wife's Full Name   ....

Birth Date   ....

Birth Place   ....

Father's Full Name   ....

Mother's Full Name   ....

Brothers & Sisters   ....

Our Children

Husband

Wife

Spouse

Spouse

Spouse

Spouse

Spouse

Spouse

Our Grandchildren

Our Descendents

Include further details of your children, grandchildren and great grandchildren (the meaning of names chosen, birthdays, time and place of birth, and any other special details).

"Children are the true connoisseurs. What's precious to them has no price, only value."

Bel Kaufman

Husband's Ancestral Chart

Husband's Paternal Grandfather

Date & Place of Birth

Husband's Father

Date & Place of Birth

Husband's Paternal Grandmother

Date & Place of Birth

Great Grandfather

Great Grandmother

Great Grandfather

Great Grandmother

Husband's Ancestral Chart

Great Great Grandfather

Great Great Grandmother

Great Great Grandfather

Great Great Grandmother

Great Great Grandfather

Great Great Grandmother

Great Great Grandfather

Great Great Grandmother

Great Great Great Grandparents

Husband's Ancestral Chart

Husband's Maternal Grandfather

Date & Place of Birth

Great Grandfather

Great Grandmother

Husband's Mother

Date & Place of Birth

Husband's Maternal Grandmother

Date & Place of Birth

Great Grandfather

Great Grandmother

Husband's Ancestral Chart

Great Great Grandfather

Great Great Grandmother

Great Great Grandfather

Great Great Grandmother

Great Great Grandfather

Great Great Grandmother

Great Great Grandfather

Great Great Grandmother

Great Great Great Grandparents

Wife's Ancestral Chart

Wife's Paternal Grandfather

Date & Place of Birth

Great Grandfather

Great Grandmother

Wife's Father

Date & Place of Birth

Wife's Paternal Grandmother

Date & Place of Birth

Great Grandfather

Great Grandmother

Wife's Ancestral Chart

Great Great Grandfather

_____

Great Great Grandmother

_____

Great Great Grandfather

_____

Great Great Grandmother

_____

Great Great Grandfather

_____

Great Great Grandmother

_____

Great Great Grandfather

_____

Great Great Grandmother

Great Great Great Grandparents

Wife's Ancestral Chart

Wife's Maternal Grandfather

Date & Place of Birth

Wife's Mother

Date & Place of Birth

Wife's Maternal Grandmother

Date & Place of Birth

Great Grandfather

Great Grandmother

Great Grandfather

Great Grandmother

Wife's Ancestral Chart

Great Great Grandfather

— — — — — — — — — — — — — —

Great Great Grandmother

— — — — — — — — — — — — — —

Great Great Grandfather

— — — — — — — — — — — — — —

Great Great Grandmother

— — — — — — — — — — — — — —

Great Great Grandfather

— — — — — — — — — — — — — —

Great Great Grandmother

— — — — — — — — — — — — — —

Great Great Grandfather

— — — — — — — — — — — — — —

Great Great Grandmother

Great Great Great Grandparents

Husband's Family

Include details of brothers and sisters and their children.

"A people without history is like wind on the buffalo grass."
Sioux Proverb

Husband's Family

Include details of aunts and uncles and cousins (father's side).

Husband's Family

Include details of aunts and uncles and cousins (mother's side).

Husband's Family

Include details of great aunts and uncles and second cousins.

Husband's Family

Wife's Family

Include details of brothers and sisters and their children.

"Remember me when I am gone away,
Gone far away into the silent land."

Christina Rossetti

Wife's Family

Include details of aunts and uncles and cousins (father's side).

Wife's Family

Include details of aunts and uncles and cousins (mother's side).

Wife's Family

Include details of great aunts and uncles and second cousins.

Wife's Family

Special Occasions

Include weddings, christenings, important birthdays and family reunions.

Special Occasions

"All who joy would win
Must share it, —
Happiness was born a Twin."

Byron: Don Juan

Special Occasions

Special Occasions

Family Homes

"The home of everyone is to him his castle and fortress, as well for his defence against injury and violence, as for his repose."

Edward Coke

Education and Special Achievements

Education and Special Achievements

"Education is what survives when what has been learnt has been forgotten."

B K Skinner

_

Business Life

"Whenever you see a successful business,
someone once made a courageous decision."

Peter Drucker

Business Life

Family Friends

Family Friends

"The ornament of a house is the friends who frequent it."
Ralph Waldo Emerson

Family Pets

"Animals are such agreeable friends – they ask no questions, they pass no criticisms."
George Eliot

Family Holidays

"What is this life if, full of care,
We have no time to stand and stare?"

W H Davies

Family Holidays

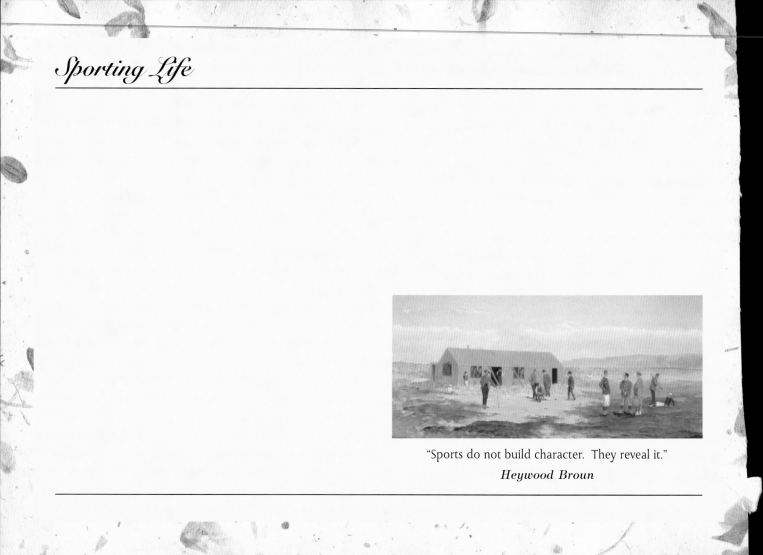

"Sports do not build character. They reveal it."

Heywood Broun

Clubs & Organisations

"I do not care to belong to a club that accepts people like me as members."
Groucho Marx

Hobbies & Interests

"To the art of working well a civilised race would add the art of playing well."

Ralph Waldo Emerson

Special Memories

Use this section for any other notes about your family, for inserting special photographs and for keeping together newspaper clippings, certificates and so forth.

Special Memories

"A man's real possession is his memory. In nothing else is he rich, in nothing else is he poor."
Alexander Smith

Special Memories

"Memory is the diary that we all carry about with us."
Oscar Wilde

Special Memories

Important Family Dates

Keep a record of your own special family calendar, including birthdays, anniversaries, traditions etc.

Date	Event	Date	Event

Printed in China by Man Sang Envelope Manufacturing Co. Ltd

Acknowledgements:
Motherhood, 1898 by Louis (Emile) Adan (1839-1937)
Waterhouse and Dodd, London/Bridgeman Art Library, London

Sweet Dreams by Thomas Brooks (1818-91)
Phillips, The International Fine Art Auctioneers/Bridgeman Art Library, London

The First, the only one by John Haynes-Williams (1836-1908)
York City Art Gallery/Bridgeman Art Library, London

May Day by James Hayllar (1829-1920)
Sotheby's Picture Library

Registering the Birth by Ralph Hedley (1851-1913)
Sotheby's Picture Library

Maternity by Beatrice Howe (20th century)
Atkinson Art Gallery, Southport, Lancs./Bridgeman Art Library, London

The Mother by Thomas Musgrave Joy (1812-66)
York City Art Gallery/Bridgeman Art Library, London

Maternity by Thomas Benjamin Kennington (1856-1916)
Sotheby's Picture Library

The Cradle, 1872 by Berthe Morisot (1841-95)
Musee d'Orsay, Paris/Bridgeman Art Library

A Mother's Darling, 1880, by Jessie McGregor D.1919
Sotheby's Picture Library

The First Tooth by Frederick Morgan (1856-1927)
Sotheby's Picture Library

Maternal Care by Evert Pieters (1856-1932)
Josef Mensing Gallery, Hamm-Rhynern/Bridgeman Art Library, London

The New Baby by Evert Pieters (1856-1932)
Private Collection/Bridgeman Art Library, London